SONG OF

Homage To John Coltrane

John Sinclair

SONG OF PRAISE
Homage To John Coltrane

John Sinclair

Trembling Pillow Press, 2011
New Orleans, LA

SONG OF PRAISE   Homage To John Coltrane
by John Sinclair

Trembling Pillow Press
New Orleans, LA
ISBN-13: 978-0-9790702-59
Copyright © 2011 John Sinclair
The John Sinclair Foundation
(Amsterdam, Detroit, London)

Typesetting and Design: Megan Burns
Cover Design: Dave Brinks
Cover Photograph of John Coltrane: Courtesy of Leni Sinclair, © 1966, 2011.
Frontispiece Photo: Ras Moshe and Daniel Carter on Saxophone with John
Sinclair performing Homage To John Coltrane: Courtesy of Eero Ruuttila
Interior Author Photo: John Sinclair broadcasting at Eat at Jo's in Melkneg,
Amsterdam: Courtesy of Jacques Morial

Trembling
Pillow
PRESS

http://tremblingpillowpress.com

SONG OF PRAISE

Homage To John Coltrane

John Sinclair

SONG OF PRAISE
Homage To John Coltrane

YOU HAD TO BE THERE

You had to be there. Words are not available fully to convey the impact of John Coltrane, his fearless musical creations and exemplary persona on the generation of musicians, artists, poets and cultural warriors that came of age in the 1960s.

You had to be there. The stiff crust of the American social order was cracking open. Black people were moving for social and political equality in a big, inspirational way. The Cuban Revolution was well under way. The President of the United States was gunned down by a hellish collective of CIA agents and Mafiosi. Artists and academics were beginning to speak out forcefully for nuclear disarmament and against the ever-burgeoning war in Vietnam.

You had to be there. White people were discovering the blues. Hippies refused to cut their hair or get a job, smoked dope and dropped acid, plugged in their guitars and played rock & roll music, resisted the military draft, dropped out of the consumer society and lived together in urban and rural communes. American poetry and creative music and art were at an all-time high point and giants of every artistic discipline walked the earth.

You had to be there. Soul music was on the radio. Black people were on the move. Martin Luther King was leading massive civil rights marches and demonstrations and sit-ins all around the country. Students were rebelling. Draft resistance was on the rise. The government was on the defensive. Malcolm X was assassinated in the middle of a sermon. Four little black girls were blown up by white racist bombs placed in a church in Alabama. Voter registration workers from SNCC and CORE were murdered by white racists in Mississippi and elsewhere in the South.

You had to be there. The music was everywhere, fresh and exciting and charged with the moment: *Freedom Suite* by Sonny Rollins, *Haitian Fight Song* and *Better Get It in Yo' Soul* by Charles Mingus, *Freedom Now* by Max Roach & Abbey Lincoln, *Let Freedom Ring* by Jackie McLean, *Change of the Century* by Ornette Coleman, *Kind of Blue* by Miles Davis, *The Heliocentric World of Sun Ra*, *Giant Steps* and *Africa/Brass* and *Out of This World* and *A Love Supreme* by John Coltrane.

You had to be there. You had to be there when the records came out. You had to be there in the little nightclubs and coffeehouses where the music was made. You had to be there where the music was and the musicians, and the people whose lives were illuminated and reshaped by the music in action. You had to be there to see and hear what was going to happen, and when it happened, and how you could be a part of it.

You had to be there. If you were looking for a way out of the American stasis and a stake in the immediate future, you had to be there. It was all there in the music, spelled out in fiery notes and relentless rhythms with ceaseless intelligence and spontaneous improvisation, and you had to be there to stand under the music and understand what it was telling you.

You had to be there. There was no other place you would want to be. You had to be there to hear and see and feel the message of freedom and immense human possibility blazed across your mental sky by the music of John Coltrane & his thrilling quartets made in America between 1959 and Trane's untimely demise in 1967. There was nothing like it then, and there's nothing like it now.

You had to be there. But since you couldn't be there, maybe this book of homages to John Coltrane in verse and prose will help give you a tiny idea of what it was about, and how it reached us, and what it made us feel and think and do as we received it and figured out how to act on it.

The poems in SONG OF PRAISE were principally composed between 1965 and 1967, inspired by specific Coltrane works from the albums: *John Coltrane Live at the Village Vanguard, Coltrane Plays the Blues, Coltrane Jazz, Crescent, Kulu Se Mama,* and *Meditations.*

The critical writings represent record reviews of the albums titled *Coltrane Live at Birdland, Crescent, A Love Supreme* and *The John Coltrane Quartet Plays* written upon their release, a report of a Coltrane concert at the *downbeat* Jazz Festival in August 1965, and a long retrospective of Trane's Atlantic years written upon the release of *The Heavyweight Champion* boxed set in the 1990s.

You had to be there. I was there. I had to be there. That was exactly where it was at, and I wouldn't have missed it for the world.

—John Sinclair
New Orleans
February 21, 2009

for Charles Moore

& the great Amiri Baraka

I

HOMAGE TO JOHN COLTRANE

"spiritual"

for linda jones

what is jazz, but spirituals
played thru saxophones
& trombones,

spirit voices
thru metal tubings
& the terrible repetition

of the formal premise, viz.
trance-like
at its best, or boring

when the spirit doth not move,
oh what is blues
but spirituals with a line

removed,
that is structurally,
& in content just a prayer

to the gods of daily life,
to ask the blessing
that the body of another

may lay warm in the bed
beside you at night, and the rent
be paid, and a meal

on the table, with the sheriff
far away
from the scene of the crime, oh

what is jazz but the registration
of the human personality
in relation to the spiritual,

stripped of literal meaning
but full of sound & portent,
direct as the voice of the gods

—Detroit
September 15, 1985

HOMAGE TO JOHN COLTRANE

For David Sandburg

1

"you are sorry you are born with ears"

or you are sorry. yr
ears. how they can become
the stuff of such lies.

how a man can stand, & fall. stand. *"a*
coil
around things."   a sound

      (or a test
of what music
can bear. a
          SCREAM

                for the time

2

"John Coltrane can do this for us":

teach us to stand
up right
in the face of the most devas-
tating insensi-

tivity. can touch us
where the hand or mouth or
eye
   can't go. can see. can be
a man. make a love
from centuries of unplumbed music
& a common metal tool
anyone can misuse.
            can make you think

"of a lot of weird & wonderful things":

yrself.

            beauty.

            love.

gold & miles

                        of trees. elvin

  jones.   murdered

dreams.   a-

                  pocalypse.

                              turtles.

  the moon (& be-
yond.

            ornette.

                        grapefruits.

  silver pendulums.

MUSIC

t i m e .

                              Screaming,
jumping up & down, moaning
for some strange new dignity

before anyone can listen. before
time. before promises,
& lies. before it all collapses
on our heads.

before it's too late

3

"If you've ever sat in a Coltrane audience,
you'll understand
what I mean."

It could happen
to you, too, a loss
of control, a be-
ginning, a reshaping
of what they've always told you
to believe, the old forms

& "music," that we've been fooled with,
the "songs" they taught you,
& lied.

when we begin to understand that
what we've been told is

how they can put us exactly
where they have to believe
we have to be

4

     man,

     if you can't *hear*,

     what *can* you do?

     yr *born*

             with ears

—Detroit
Spring 1965

Quotations in italics from LeRoi Jones's liner notes to
Coltrane Live At Birdland (Impulse Records)

"blues to elvin"

born with ears, even now, packed with garbage. the stuff
of dead men. wax, & elbows.   sewage, seaweed, debris
of forgotten oceans, or shells. or
the shells & shit they beat the indians with.

for us to shut up, what they can offer. pitiful. so
small, can it bend the ear. paper, & shells. to fill
our ears, to make us forget. to sing,
made some improbable proposition. to get thru,

some genius we wanted to cry, to the moon, like
weird wolves of illusion. insanity. the stoppage.
drained, & collapse, on the floor, thru, with love, & un-
settled ears. to begin to go, where the music goes, out, to you

—Detroit
Spring 1965

"some other blues"

for james semark

what do i have
to do, spell
it all out for you? "let my

poems be a
graph of me," & with
the poems, what other
actions (gestures) i make.

"it starts out like
'now's the time' &
turns into" whatever you
make it. if you can't make

yr own way, what
ever can i tell you.
who are you. where did you
come from, to get

this way. or
this far. how did you
ever make it. (& if you can't
make these changes,

make yr own. & if these ain't
yr blues, try "something
else." this is the change
of the century. (dig it

—*Detroit*
Spring 1965

"like Sonny,"

like Ornette, like anyone
who takes himself
into the jungle of e-
motion, feeling, judge-

ments. find yrself some morning,
wake up at noon. the heat
that you feel, is yr own. the
friction, of movement. burning yr-

self up, out here, where the rain comes
too late, to save you. go away, run a-
way, back to (wherever it is
you came from. if you can stay there,

forget it. if you can
move, come out. if
you can stand it. this is really
where it's at. (motives

—*Detroit*
May 6, 1965

"the drum thing"

for danny spencer, ronnie johnson, & don moye

caught between, drums (one set

to the side, as one is

above, blowing, as the other, measured, rolls

above me the horn is

played, for the ear, where i

live, here, with a drum aside (either side

of my head. as the music

defines this, our

home, here, where we play this (day

by day, the horns, drum, the music

in my head, as the broken pulse,

smooth pulse, the music, moves thru my head. as the

words, sing themselves, to the page. as

music

—Detroit
Spring 1965

"blues to you"

for danny spencer

we wanted them to love us,
as a first term. to know that we knew,
& would tell them with our eyes,
& our pumping feet. would sit & stare

at the bandstand
or at each other, & grin. or get up from the chair
& walk smack into a pole
after 45 minutes of elvin jones. john coltrane

was a hero beyond legend, i mean
he was right there in front of us, right there
where we could see him, & know for ever
the whole thing was real.

or sit for days, literally days,
& play the records through our meat, & dream
of touching them, the musicians,
as they walked off the stand, & moved past us,

smiling, toward some secret place
we would never go. & loved them always
for a simple nod, as if we were really real.
we needed them to speak to us

of pure revolution. to put down their saxophones
& spout pure poetry, or our lives
weren't shit. were gobs of dream
splattered against the world.

oh we were young
& made of america. it made us
what we were. & are. &, if we are lucky,
we will live through it all. yes, & the music

will ring in our ears. & we will hear it,
& it will bring us through. we will wake up
singing
of a world of our own. a world

where they will love us, just as if
(& only if)
we are as real
as they are

—Detroit
January 3, 1967/
New Orleans
December 22, 1993

"I Talk with the Spirits"

after Rahsaan Roland Kirk

"The hand of John Coltrane
seems never to have stopped
guiding his family,"
says Leonard Feather,
quoting Alice McLeod Coltrane
in the *Los Angeles Times*, July 25, 1982:

"Just two or three years ago
there was a definite conver-
sation with him,
while I was in a meditative state,
on the subject of life
after death, & living

in the particular existence
that he's in. I noticed
that he did have an instrument—
it looked something
like a soprano, but much
longer

& larger—& he was
quite absorbed
with looking at its structure.
I asked him, 'Do you think
about Earth life?' He said,
'*not much.*' I said,

'Do you consider
that you might prefer
living on Earth
as opposed to your life
in the afterlife?' & he said,
'*No,*

*I wouldn't prefer
living on Earth.*' So I said,
'Really? Not with all
the acceptance, the
recognition, the fame?'
His reply was, '*I prefer*

> *the Spirit*
> *life*
> *to the way*
> *life*
> *is*
> *on Earth*'"

—Detroit
August, 1982

II

SONG OF PRAISE

"Song of Praise"

Sing the song then, let it sound
through the land. The song that now
keeps us alive, when the other noise

is there to kill us, to deaden our ears
to the song of our selves that
these musicians sing. Let the force of it

make its way into our hearts
in the last days of this era,
this error less human men have made

of our time. The time is now, that we can make
a true song of our selves, a music that will
open all of our I's to each

other. Let such a man as
Jimmy Garrison be your base, you can
build on a music strong as his

& make your time as free as
Elvin's, your touch as McCoy's, your song as
pure as Trane's, sing a song

as strong as theirs, a song of praise
for every body on earth, & for the love
of all of our selves—

a song to lead us on
in this cold december
of a long & murderous year

—Detroit
December 6, 1965/
New Orleans
December 4, 1995

John Coltrane Quartet
COLTRANE LIVE AT BIRDLAND
Impulse A-50

John Coltrane, tenor & soprano saxophones; McCoy Tyner,
piano; Jimmy Garrison, bass; Elvin Jones, drums "Afro-Blue";
"I Want To Talk About You"; "The Promise";
"Alabama"; "Your Lady"
Recorded 1963

Bob Thiele should be arrested. Along with John, McCoy, Jimmy
& Elvin. Records like this one (& there aren't many) are really
dangerous. Maybe Impulse should put a "warning" sign on the
jacket to keep the record company in the clear. All the tunes
are mind- twisters: listen to what Trane does in the middle of
"Alabama," the sudden suspension of sound left me crawling
around on the floor looking for my head. . .

"Afro-Blue," in the same general bag as "My Favorite Things"
and "Greensleeves" but infinitely more powerful than either,
grabs one's ears, one's soul, one's very *being*, & throws it around
the room, up against the walls, the floor, the ceiling, up, down,
around & around until you start screaming & clawing to get
out. Coltrane plays the head & turns it over to McCoy, Jimmy
& Elvin until they've got you trapped in their whirling vortex
of sound; then Elvin whips Trane in with an eyes-closed,
pounding, splattering orgasm of sound, screaming, crying,
blasting, shouting, with the Emperor Jones bullying & pushing
& crashing all under & over everyone else.

Not satisfied with this total victory, Trane begins an unbelievable "I Want To Talk About You" that sums up his five years' work since the Prestige version (on *Soultrane*, LP 7142) was cut; his virtuoso *a capella* cadenza should make tenor players want to sell their horns. "The Promise" is really a fulfillment of all the promises Trane has made (& kept) in the past: beautiful & shattering, it's the loveliest promise I've ever been made.

"Alabama," as LeRoi Jones says in his hallucinogenic liner notes, is a beautiful *word*, but nothing to Trane's devastating playing, with Jimmy moaning away underneath him & Elvin driving through the Alabama night, through the mist & tears, through minds & hearts & loves, pleading, cajoling, caressing, forgiving, loving. . . And "Your Lady" is, to quote Jones again, a "lovely" tune, & the four brothers are themselves lovely in their interpretation of its peculiar beauty.

Love, in fact, has a lot to do with these men & their music. The Quartet has been together now for a full two years, working continually to produce some of the most significant music of our time. McCoy Tyner is in the very first rank of modern pianists, & he plays on this record at levels he has seldom reached before. Jimmy Garrison, pitifully underrated, plays so much bass it's a shame; he's always right *there* with the choicest, juiciest notes, fitting his big fat sound into the group gestalt without a flaw.

And Elvin & Trane! They whip each other into frenzies of creativity & love & pure musical genius like no one has ever heard. The closest parallel I can think of is the remarkable partnership of Ravi Shankar & Chatur Lal, the Indian *virtuosi*. Trane & Elvin are (as has been noted) often evocative of this profoundly exciting, strangely hypnotic pair of master musicians; their own mastery is in fact at an equal level with their Eastern counterparts.

To quote LeRoi Jones once again (& his notes alone are almost worth the price of the album): "If you can hear, this music will make you think of a lot of weird & wonderful things. You might even become one of them."

—Detroit
Spring 1964

John Coltrane Ouartet
CRESCENT
lmpulse A-66

John Coltrane, tenor saxophone; McCoy Tyner, piano;
Jimmy Garrison, bass; Elvin Jones, drums
"Crescent"; "Wise One"; "Bessie's Blues"; "Lonnie's Lament";
"The Drum Thing"
Recorded April 27 and June 1, 1964

Crescent is like the other side of the *Birdland* record: the darker side of an opulent moon, the side people blinded by some other light can't see: an extension of light into darker, somehow richer areas of consciousness.

Crescent is the portion of Coltrane's music that everyone who has been listening to him over the last four years already knows about, thoroughly, and loves, too; but the part that can perhaps get to his less open auditors easier than, say, the *Birdland* or the *Impressions* albums.

And the new recording is every bit as much a group music as the others, but in a different (more subtle) sense. While "Afro-Blue"demands a total group involvement on the intensest emotional level from each of the four men– total in the sense that each man must immerse himself completely, at the farthest reaches of his own musical capability and complexity, in the torrent of the total musical creation–the music collected in the *Crescent* album commands each man's unrelenting cooperation in the creation of a more quietly intense, more subtly profound beauty.

Like the difference in nuance of intensity between, say, the bright day sun's light and the concentrated glow of a single candle in a midnight room: the sun blasts its warmth at the all-too-ready senses, the candle burns its deep heat more into the darkest labyrinths of the brain itself, somehow transcending the physical senses (though certainly not short-circuiting them) for the pure concave plane of the mind.

Within the group itself each man takes his place as an equal with the others, each as responsible as the next for the final musical result. The ideal group situation exists in Coltrane's band: the four musicians uncompromisingly complement each other, they stimulate one another to play at all times the maximum music of which they are capable in the given context.

In *Crescent*, the tunes were conceived by Trane (they're all his own compositions) as showcases not only for the group as a whole but for each individual in the group. Where we usually hear only Trane and McCoy in "solo", here Jimmy ("Lonnie's Lament") and Elvin ("The Drum Thing") each have a tune virtually all to themselves, with warmly sincere introductory endorsements by John and McCoy.

Trane's main tune is "Crescent": while the group assigns itself what seems primarily a supporting role, John pushes himself farther and farther into the music, creating a full-blooded monument to beauty and life that can't be crumbled by any man's insensitivity. His solo twists and turns, he worries a phrase, strokes it, caresses, pushes and pulls at it until it gives up and turns into another phrase to be made love to. Each statement leads irrevocably to the next, fatally, in an unquestionable logic that is only Coltrane's and only our own.

He does the same thing to "Wise One." After a gently explored introduction, Elvin urges Trane in with the most beautiful cymbal work I've ever heard, creating an elegant spectrum of gold-bathed color that brings itself into focus on Coltrane's genius as it spreads into Elvin's rare and unequaled ride, carrying Trane with it and beyond it, far, far, into the splendid Persian vault of his mind where we see its lavish tapestries, jars of frankincense and myrrh, acres and acres of purest gold and deep unmined silver, row on row of unsurpassed diamonds and emeralds, a wealth of gleaming rubies and deep smoked pearls.

While "Bessie's Blues" is Bessie Smith 1964 Coltrane style, the same old blues he always plays, with everything all four of them know about the blues crystallized in this reaffirmation of the blues as a not-so-unnecessary part of everything total living is. McCoy gets his shot here and chases those old dastards up and down his very own keyboard and throws them to Trane to throw away for any old day you listen to this record.

On "Lonnie's Lament" Jimmy Garrison defines the bass solo for right now, and his brother Elvin redefines drums and drumming for this time around (don't he always?) on "The Drum Thing", bringing all his awareness of every piece of his set and everything each piece can do into his own wildly controlled contemporary focus.

This record is an indispensable document in the case for John Coltrane's all-faceted genius. The music speaks for itself: listen to it. See for yourself.

−Detroit
January 1965

John Coltrane Quartet
A LOVE SUPREME
Impulse A-77

John Coltrane, tenor & soprano saxophones; McCoy Tyner,
piano; Jimmy Garrison, bass; Elvin Jones, drums
"A Love Supreme": Part I—Acknowledgement;
Part II—Resolution; Part III—Pursuance; Part IV—Psalm
Recorded December 9, 1964

*Each new album he produces, it seems to me, in all likelihood
will be a major exhibit in the continuity of his artistic growth.
There are very few artists in any field whose every work is of
interest. John Coltrane is one.*

—Ralph J. Gleason,
Liner Notes to *Ole Coltrane* (1961)

A Love Supreme is an enormous musical, emotional,
personal statement by a genius of modern music. The
continuing record we have, of John Coltrane's music, is an
index to the development of an *artist* of gigantic stature, &
it can be taken as an immediately useful model for anyone,
of whatever persuasion, who is looking to grow, to extend
the limits of consciousness as far as they will go. How John
Coltrane found himself, & took what he found of himself,
into himself, & brought it back out, thru himself, to us. *A
Love Supreme* shows us where he is now, & why, & even

how. It is of the greatest interest, to you, if you are at all *interested* in yourself & what John Coltrane has to do with you.

With his latest recording, Coltrane has moved into a freer, more *open* music than many of us had thought possible for him. What he has done, now, is to begin to analyze emotional states through his music. Up to this record he moved mainly to create emotion, & to transmit it, thru energy, to you, to create an emotional involvement, there, out of your own energies, as listener.

Trane has deposited "possible feeling" for you to pick up on, for you to *use*. It has up to now been your own choice, to use it or to waste it, that's been up to you. Now he has withdrawn a step, abstracted, removed himself from that close one-to-one relationship with you, in order to tell a story, of himself, how he has grown to be able to tell the story, thru his own forms, to you & for you. *A Love Supreme* is Coltrane's own biography, his *auto*biography, of himself & from himself, how he has made it, & with what help.

The process thru which Coltrane has come to this point is available to anyone with ears. I divide it up this way:

Stage 1—getting to himself, because he had to, that was when he came up, in that time when a man had to work into himself thru the forms that were left him (the records with Miles, then Monk, & back with Miles, for *Kind of Blue*, etc.);

Stage 2—getting *into* himself, to find out where he was at, & what to do with what he found (the Prestige quartet & quintet sides, circa 1958, the Atlantic sides 1959- 61—*Giant Steps, Coltrane Jazz*, then the breakthrough on *My Favorite Things, Coltrane Plays The Blues, Ole Coltrane*);

Stage 3—coming out of himself, to *create* feeling, not merely mirror it (which is where most artists had stopped, up to that time, altho a few—Ornette, Cecil Taylor— had begun to find the way out)—this starts for me with "Chasin' The Trane," "Out of This World," "Impressions" & "India," "Afro-Blue," etc.;

Stage 4—*refining* feeling, which takes place at the same time as the creation of it, *e.g.*, "Soul Eyes," the albums with Duke Ellington & Johnny Hartman—especially "Lush Life," "Autumn Serenade"—and the *Ballads* album, "After The Rain," "Alabama," & the ultimate refinements of the *Crescent* LP, especially "Crescent," "Wise One," "Bessie's Blues";

& *Stage 5* (so far)—moving into a *personal* music, creating his own forms, with which to create feeling, & move it, out, to you, into *music*, of the highest order. His own—*A Love Supreme*, how to tell his own story, his very own way.

Coltrane's example is unique because he is the only second-generation (*i.e.*, after Bird) musician who has reached this level with such intensity & emotion created & communicated during the process—although it can easily be argued that, say, Sonny Rollins &/or Charles Mingus are not far behind—there are indications of their singularity (*Our Man In Jazz, Black Saint & The Sinner Lady*) but not of the magnitude of *A Love Supreme*.

Of the creators of his generation, Miles Davis is once again simultaneously creating & refining, tho he may never really get *out* of himself; Monk is refining; Rollins & Mingus; George Russell; not many more—maybe Jackie McLean, tho of a lesser magnitude, etc.

Of the third generation: Ornette Coleman, Cecil Taylor, now Archie Shepp, John Tchicai & company, for whom such a "system" of measurement may be totally irrelevant, as they had not the intense period of finding a way to themselves that Coltrane had, they came into music without the burden of the immediate past/present to cope with, they had somehow gotten under that, were not stuck with it, as Trane was.

In this connection I find LeRoi Jones's postulation of Coltrane as Ornette & Cecil's "hired assassin" valuable: "[Coltrane] is using the various post-bop reactions to prepare, as it were, an area for Taylor & Coleman...

Coltrane's salvation will come only as a murderer, an anarchist, whose anarchy seems so radical because references to the 'old music' still remain" (*Kulchur #8*).

Which is only to say, that the new musicians, because of Trane's work, will have to waste less time getting *into* themselves, & can spend what little time they do have, on getting what is there, as themselves, out, to you—the real business they have to do.

The newer musicians, in fact, will find this measurement unnecessary, as implied above, & not of much essential use in working out their own destinies, but for Coltrane's generation it is a matter of fact, *i.e.*, it is what has actually happened.

That Coltrane has made it, to himself, & out through, is a simple measure of his genius; that he has created so much *music* in the process, is an even more convincing measure. He is now on the way to creating what is completely his *own* music, *i.e.*, without the references to the "old music" he still retained.

A Love Supreme, then, is in many ways the end of the road John has been traveling these many years, & the beginning of the new road, that will take him where he has wanted for so long to go. And there is a bigger & better place for you, as listener, on that new road, if you can bring yourself to move with him.

Coltrane, in the past few years (Stages 3 & 4) has, more than any of his contemporaries, left a place for the serious listener to get into the music; the more you bring to Trane's music, as has always been the rule, the more you will take back from it. On any level. This is what has always excited me about Coltrane's music, & about the music of the whole "third generation," that I have been rewarded in direct proportion to what I have taken to it—feeling for feeling, idea for idea. It is not "entertainment," no, not in the casual sense that word is meant, but rather enlightenment. A new concept, it seems, in jazz as art.

Given the atrophied sensibilities most Americans take to whatever art they bother with, it is not surprising to find that they are as easily satisfied as they loudly claim to be, whether as artists or as members of audiences. But John Coltrane has somehow found his way out of the artistic dead-end Americans are taught to accept—I always consider it miraculous that any of us ever escape this brainwash, heavy as it is—has transcended it, & has moved beyond reaction to creativity & self-expression, which takes us back, specifically, to *A Love Supreme*.

The music that is *A Love Supreme* is the most ambitious Trane has yet undertaken: He has moved beyond "song-form" (i.e., blues or popular melody) into his own personal form, a form that rises up out of his own experience to transform that experience into melody, into *music*.

There are no "tunes" on this record, only four "parts" of a total composition. Trane has heretofore always been a "tune player"—possibly the very best of that genre—& has consequently been limited by the song-form, limited to expressing the ideas & emotions that form(s) suggests, even though he has extended the uses of the traditional forms farther than any other musician extant.

No matter how far he has brought himself within the predetermined shape of the song-form, now that he has begun to make his own forms he has another & wholly open field in which to work. His mastery of traditional forms is complete, & he has found, as have many other artists of different disciplines, that these made-up forms are not adequate for complete self-expression, *i.e.*, once one's self has gone beyond the forms it has been told define its limits.

So Trane has moved, finally, to create his forms for his content, & to stop trying to "fit" his ideas into anyone else's shapes. Not that there's really anything wrong with them, they're just not adequate for an expanded vision, tho they still can be put to one's own use when they fit the occasion—not vice versa.

That *A Love Supreme* makes the most powerful (& accurate) registration of Coltrane's genius yet, can be offered as proof of the validity of his new method. *E.g.*, "Pursuance" reaches a point (just before the end of John's solo) when his emotional force is almost unbearable to listen to, so precisely is it registered. And the "Psalm" section of the composition communicates the same emotion on a highly-abstract level, something of which the song-form was incapable.

In his new "open" or "projective" music (to use two terms which the poet Charles Olson has applied to the analogous "movement" in contemporary American poetry), Coltrane can make new forms that are direct extensions of his musical content. He no longer (now that he's hip to it) has to try to fit his "content" into predetermined forms, no matter how many alterations or extensions of them he might have made (*e.g.*, in "Out of This World," where he reduced the normal chord sequence to two repeated chords for his harmonic base—his trademark of late, from "My Favorite Things" to now, & a technique that is made use of on the first section of *A Love Supreme*, as an example of how whatever forms there are can be put to use by the artist when he is in control of his art).

Another determining factor in the growth of Coltrane's music has been the rhythm section—McCoy Tyner, Jimmy Garrison, Elvin Jones—that has been with him steadily for the past three and a half years, growing along with him, working through the same progressions that he has until, now, the rest of the Quartet is ready to move into its own music as Coltrane has moved into his.

Jimmy & Elvin are as free now as they will ever need to be, they can—& want to—play every bit as much as Trane, & do. McCoy, who has become the most limited member of the group in its new sense only because his own music is so strongly tied to the "old music," is now too moving into new areas of piano music, but he actually has the farthest to go, of the four. When he frees himself from the modal force that presently organizes his playing, & moves into free expression on the piano (virtually an untapped instrument for new music, with the exception of Cecil & only a very few others), the whole group will be ready to make some exceedingly personal registrations. What they are now set to do to people's heads shouldn't be allowed— but thank God it is.

And "thank God" is just what John Coltrane & group do on *A Love Supreme*. Don't let the religious connection Coltrane makes bother you at all—you should rejoice in it. Coltrane has chosen to term the huge *love* in him God, & he pays homage to it (Him) in this record. *A Love Supreme* is soul music, John Coltrane's soul—love music, free music, they're all the same thing. The composition moves from a religious base ("Acknowledgement"), into its resolution ("Resolution"), to the reality aspect—the blues ("Pursuance"), to abstractions of the totality ("Psalm")—as Charles Moore puts it, "Life Love (Living Music)."

But I don't need to talk more about the music, in a specific sense, it's all there, on the record, for everyone to hear, where you can get at it. Just listen to it, that's all you need to do. John Coltrane loves you enough to give it to you— take it. HEAR!

—*Detroit*
Winter-Spring 1965

THE JOHN COLTRANE QUARTET PLAYS
Impulse A-86

John Coltrane, tenor & soprano saxophones; McCoy Tyner,
piano; Jimmy Garrison, bass; Elvin Jones, drums
"Chim Chim Cheree"; "Song of Praise"; "Nature Boy"; "Brazilia"
Add Art Davis, bass, on "Nature Boy"

It seems to me that there shouldn't need to be much
said about John Coltrane's music anymore: a new
record's released, Impulse puts its ad in *downbeat*, & then
everybody just goes out to the store & brings the record
back home & listens to it.

It should be as simple as that. Like anyone with ears
knows (or, at least, *should* know) what John's been doing
all these years, what a tremendous & singular beauty he's
been creating, & how this beauty increases daily.

But folks are so obtuse that literally thousands &
thousands of words still have to be written "about" John's
music, & still huge confusion & misunderstanding exist
as to these men's motives, needs, & actual *music*. That fact
speaks clearer than anything else—even more clearly than
say, the music itself—of the jungle of chaos this world
we "live" in has become. When even the most benevolent
& illuminating voices out here are taken for something
other than what they in fact are—words of love, sounds of
beauty.

I write out of need—it's that simple—I write because I need to write, on whatever level, as, it makes living in this world possible. John Coltrane's music likewise comes out of that need, & likewise makes a life possible, for him, as maker, as well as for me, listening, here, wherever I am.

John Coltrane's music suggests possibilities of feeling, emotion, thought—of life finally—that we all of us can make use of—& should. Any other use of his music is specious.

Coltrane's total commitment to himself & his art—his *music*—of which we have the most concrete evidence imaginable, *i.e.* his recordings & his nightly work before audiences everywhere—is one of the most valuable and useful tools we have.

> *"John Coltrane can do this for us"*:
>
> teach us to stand
> up right
> in the face of the most devas-
> tating insensi-
> tivity. can touch us
> where the hand or mouth or
> eye
>   can't go. can see. can be
> a man. make a love

> from centuries of unplumbed music
> & a common metal tool
> anyone can misuse.

The tool John Coltrane has made of his music is as accessible to us as our selves are. As, say, "Chim Chim Cheree" is, which serves—like Archie Shepp's "Girl From Ipanema"—as a valuable lesson in the use of whatever materials exist, in whatever form, for one's own purposes. Or, as Walt Disney made the song available, as "music" for one of his obscene films, John Coltrane found it & made actual living music out of it. As we all can, from whatever silly objects we find in front of us, in this world.

"Nature Boy" too, had already found an existence for itself in this world, & made itself useful to us before as a thing of rather simple beauty, *e.g.*, in Nat Cole's & Miles Davis's songs of it. "Once there was a boy / a very strange en- / chanted boy," etc. Then John Coltrane:

> took this boy, be-
> came this boy, &
>
> disappeared
>
> into the actual jungle
> of that boy's "nature"
>
> Hear Art Davis & Jimmy Garrison in-
> vent this nature, this

jungle, make it real, as
Elvin & McCoy do, as

Trane does, as he ex-
plores it, the "jungle of e-
motion, feeling, judge-

ments," the
mind of this boy, his
nature, that of

all of us

"Nature Boy" is some of the most amazing music this
group has ever made. "Brazilia" & "Song of Praise" too, &
let me here just advertise Jimmy Garrison's bass work on
the latter—he plays there, as he does so much now, as if
on a guitar, his instrument is that accessible to him. As his
mind is. As our selves are.

Enough. But let me just say that if you know & love John
Coltrane's music as I do, this latest recording will come
as no surprise, & you will take it to heart—straight to
heart—as I have. If you don't know John Coltrane's music,
you can start here, or anywhere. If you don't *love* John
Coltrane's music, then:

what
ever can i tell you.

who are you. where did you
come from, to get

this way. or
this far. how did you
ever make it.

—Detroit
September 1965

CECIL TAYLOR, JOHN COLTRANE & ARCHIE SHEPP

At the *downbeat* Jazz Festival
Chicago, August 15, 1965

Most of the attractions at the *downbeat* Jazz Festival were pretty much standard summer fare, and the audiences (& critics) handled them in the usual way, being impressed by mediocrities (Gary McFarland, Joe Daley, Bunky Green, *et al*) and scared off by any strength that made itself felt in anyone's music (Cecil, Trane, Shepp).

Cecil Taylor, John Coltrane & Archie Shepp brought a strength & power to Chicago that was so huge & direct that you could see these other folks *cringe* in fear of it, of what it might do to them—make them FEEL. Take them out of the life that had been proposed for them, into a reality of their own, where they can make themselves over in their *own* image.

Our people (*i.e.*, Americans white & black) have gone that far from themselves that when such a giant fund of "possible feeling" is offered them, by musicians such as these, they can't take it and they run away from it; they are that scared.

I don't know any other way to put it. Cecil Taylor's quartet (with Jimmy Lyons, Henry Grimes and Andrew Cyrille) finished off the afternoon concert, following a lot of bebop by groups of tired Chicago players and a watered-down, obscene exhibition by the "avant–garde" group Chicago is priding itself on, the Joe Daley Trio.

Cecil opened with a piece that utilized his plucking of the piano's strings and clacking with a set of brightly-colored cylindrical wooden sticks—a nice mood-setter. After thus introducing himself to the waning afternoon audience—there were probably 200 people left—Taylor moved to the piano bench and proceeded to make some of the strongest music I've ever heard.

But there were contrary reports afterwards, and weird put-downs, *e.g.* Wayne Jones, in *Coda*, October / November 1965:

"In his second selection, Mr. Taylor played the keyboard of the piano, lunging around on the bench and banging out dissonances up and down. His cohorts added chaos and mayhem of their own. A few favoured souls, dressed as railroadmen or lumberjacks, with beards and wild eyes, could be seen bobbing and chuckling aloud during this melee, and doubtless it was comforting to them. Me, I go for that old stuff, and I wasn't sorry I had to leave early. Sure, Cecil, you're just ahead of your time, that's all it is."

Yeah, well, I was one of those "favoured souls," and the man's right, it was very comforting for us to hear a man making some *music* that afternoon, after we had driven all the way over there from Detroit, given all our money—every dollar we had—to the cops in Hammond, Indiana who were running a speed trap on the way, sat through all the bullshit that preceded Taylor's set, and then Cecil made up for all that, & everything else bad that had gone on before, with a music so strong & unique that it is without match anywhere in the world. I am writing now more than three months after that day, but there was music played that afternoon & responses to it in my own being that I will never forget.

Cecil was at the center of my attention—Jimmy Lyons was nice, Henry Grimes is, simply, a *bitch*, & Cyrille took care of plenty business—but Cecil was, for my ears, the single FOCUS, the *commanding* musician. He has come up with one of the most precise & total musics ever imagined. There is nothing of "experimentation" in it—his music is a whole, mature, fully-realized thing, & to call it merely "experiment" (as most tradition-bound ears are given to doing) is to miss the whole point of what he has done.

What comes closest to me in Cecil's music is his exploitation of his instrument, *all* of it, & the possibilities for the exploitation of feeling & intellection his use of the piano opens up for him, his musicians, & his listeners. There is no sloppiness whatsoever in Cecil's playing, no shucking & jiving, no falling back on someone else's music or musics—he is working in what is called in poetry the "open field," where the shape of the music is created from moment to moment by the force of the matter (feeling/ intellection) as it comes to the player & out through him, into his instrument & out through *that*, to the hearer, to likewise shape *his* own reality.

It is the basis of Cecil Taylor's strength that he works in this "open field" at all points, but what he *does* in that field is really the point, what takes it beyond "experimentation" (the player realizing that such an open field is a possibility for him) & into pure *creation*—functioning in the field, making your *own* registrations there, exploiting & mastering your own equipment & bringing it into use for your own ends, whatever they might come to be.

Cecil is playing now, *three years after* his most recent record release, a music so strong & complete that it "will make the finger-poppers shudder," as LeRoi Jones put it. Because what Cecil does, & what he did that afternoon in Chicago, is create a music that moves straight from himself, through his precise and powerful articulation of the complex living thing he has found himself to be, to you, to your own sense of emotion/intellection, & with unrelenting accuracy & determination he forces movement at you which, if you are at all open to him, will move you to new definitions & senses of what you are, & what everything is, all about.

Cecil Taylor is not AHEAD of his time, he is precisely OF it, IN this beautiful time, a time which is beautiful only because such men as Cecil Taylor, John Coltrane & Archie Shepp are here with it, trying to pull your coat to your self.

****

The Sunday night show opened with Gary McFarland's fey ensemble, followed with the Thelonious Monk Quartet and a Roy Eldridge-Gerry Mulligan collaboration over the Monk rhythm section and pianist Ray Bryant. Then the heavyweights came on stage, John Archie McCoy Jimmy & Elvin, & the faithful (what few of us there were) moved up to the front under the lip of the stage, ducking the attendants charged with keeping everything orderly.

But what arbitrarily enforced order obtained was quickly shattered: Trane & the band established their presence with a stately out-of-tempo entrance, moving out of traditionally-measured time as they have been doing lately, & then Shepp literally *took over*, forcing his own hard mashing music on the group, and after a minute or two (Tyner & Garrison, having found themselves in the way of the music, laid out) there were only Shepp & Jones, blasting all intellection out of existence, opening up huge reservoirs of PURE FEELING in themselves & in us.

Their music was so strong people were *stunned* by the force of it. Shepp played as if plugged into the main current of energy & motion in himself, he tapped the source of all feeling & moved straight out from there, & even Elvin couldn't keep up with him. He was that fast & direct & out of himself. Shepp washed out everyone's stopped-up minds & ears, & those who wouldn't give up their egos to this music were forced back against a wall of fear & terror that was on the verge of crumbling down on their heads.

McCoy Tyner took over then & saved them with his attempt to restore some semblance of recognizable structure, but there were still enough random energy vectors filling up the night that he really had to wrestle with it, & Archie's huge vibrations carried so much after-image that they would creep into Tyner's playing & try to distort it.

Tyner gave it up to Jimmy Garrison, who moved to another level of time/space altogether & disappeared totally into his instrument, making himself one with it, creating a body of sound most of us would have thought alien to his bass had he not proved us liars there on the spot.

When Trane came back in, though, he shot everyone straight back to where Shepp had left off & took it from there, straight into places in his own being that I doubt even *he* knew existed before that moment, using every possibility his horribly inadequate tenor saxophone afforded—screaming & howling, crying shouting cursing moaning wailing until any preconceived ideas of "music" that had been in our minds were blown to bits & we had to take him on his own terms, wholly as he had taken himself then, without artifice or any other form of lie—PURE FEELING, PURE EXPRESSION, PURE MOVEMENT, like nothing I've ever heard or dreamed of.

It was a frightening experience—I looked around & saw people shaking, trembling, jaws dropped, mouths agape, their eyes glazed, & heard myself screaming with Trane, SCREAMING, jumping up & down, rolling on the ground, then past that & laughing & shouting, given a whole new sense of my self & what my own possibilities for feeling were, my possibilities for living as my self, no one else, just that.

Archie had already been though all this before, it was no surprise to him as it seemed to Trane, he stood there unblinking hearing Trane tear into himself so, & when he heard Trane pass his worst point Shepp joined in with him, head to head, in one of the most shattering musical experiences I've ever had in my life. There was energy enough created on that stage in those last 10 minutes to blow up the earth, & yet these men were using that vast store of feeling for *human* purposes, as a means of self-expression & catharsis, to raise us above the plain of suffering & struggle to where we can feel & tap into the energy & potential that are blocked by the vicissitudes of daily life.

Let me repeat: I have never heard anything like the music these men made there that night, even as many times as I've left a Coltrane performance completely blown apart, literally staggering, trying to fit the pieces I've found of myself back together in some human order—& there's nothing like it on record.

I will say only, in testimony, that I hope the rest of my life, whatever act I can make of it, will serve as proof of the power of the music I heard that night in Chicago—and that everything I do, as everything these musicians do, is done with this goal in mind, that people of this earth may someday come to see themselves as what they are, infinite human beings, with no limits but those they place upon themselves, & that all will at last step out into the world of infinite possibilities that is there now, waiting for us to use it.

—Detroit
November 30, 1965

"sing the song"

for marion sunny sinclair

sing the song a-
gain, we are gaining on it,
looks like every day now
the sun will shine a-

gain, the seasons
change, the seed with-
in the woman
swells & grows to

live within us all,
the seed within *our* earth
is the seed of all life,
all song is in the air,

the seasons change again,
the song will change,
our lives will change,
the changes will move us

as the music moves us, we
raise our lives to the sun
& sing of it, sing change, sing
the new year in,

it is ours

—Detroit
December 16, 1967/
Amsterdam
March 23, 2008

III

MEDITATIONS

"Consequences"

The music moves inside my self,
I mean I feel saxophones in-
side my meat, a force in-
spiring that meat
to sing pure electricity. Flashes. Scream,

Move out from the wall
of your self. Out from there,
Now, or you stay there. What you thought
that man was screaming, that he wanted
to get inside you. "You," again, like some stupid
broken record.

              The music moves inside,
& stays there. A part of what you are. & NOT
"from." But the song of meat energy
burning to come through you.   In charge.   & that energy
makes its way. Yes, shapes it, & is in charge. *In,*
goddamnit, IN the meat,
and *of* it. Yes,

yes, yes. A
firming it. And where you can go
to find that one place, I mean
it *is* the meat. And the song
that moves that self, & shapes it, ah, ah,

well yes it does

—*Detroit*
December 20, 1966

"Welcome"

is that feeling you have
when you finally do reach an awareness,
an understanding which you have earned through struggle. It is a
feeling of peace. A welcome
feeling of peace.

—John Coltrane

Welcome.

Please come in &
have a seat with us. Break bread. Yes. Sit with us,
hold the hand of that human
being next to you. Yes. You have come

a long long way,
we can see it in your eyes. And the way you stand,
the human grace that marks your movements.
Yes. Welcome. We have been

waiting for you. It is time you came to us.
Yes. It is time
for all to come. It is a time now
when all *can* come, to sit with us,

to sit with us in peace. You have come through
the hardest part, & you know it. Yes. You can
feel it. You wear it in your cells. Yes. Please,

break bread with us. A little rice. And pass
the pipe there
to your friend. Yes. And now we will sing,

we will sing together,
we will sing the song of our lives—

Yes.   Yes.   Yes.   Yes.   Yes.

Yes

       Yes

          Yes

             Yes

Yes

       Yes

              Yes

                 Yes

        YES

—Detroit
February 9, 1967

"Vigil"

implies watchfulness. Anyone tring to attain perfection
is faced with various obstacles in life which tend to sidetrack him.
Here, therefore, I mean watchfulness against elements that might be
destructive— from within or without.

—John Coltrane

There are forces that will move against you even though
the world is yours. You must watch for them, all ways,
even though you should not have to. They will move

in ways you will not know,
for you are pure, & their movement
is not as yours is, straight & direct, as you move

all ways through the world. Oh they will strike you
as you move to grow, they will knock you down,
they will kick you in the face & smile,

they will have you understand
that the world is not yours, it is theirs they say, & you will
not know why they would have you die a

death like theirs, no, you will not come to
understand them, & they will keep at you. They will call
you their enemy, even though you know not

what an enemy is, you are not bent, you are straight,
straight & open to their blows, you cannot know
that they get their kicks that way, you go your own way

& it is good, it is only natural that you do, "I don't try
to set standards of perfection
for anyone else. I do feel

everyone does try to reach
his better self, his full potential, & what that consists of
depends on each individual. Whatever that goal is,

moving toward it does require vigilance."
& you will watch for them,
you will be vigilant,

because you have to. You do what you have to. You are a
meat creature, moving in the world. You will move
as you have to move,

& they will move to stop you. You can not be stopped.
They do not know that, & they will move against you.
Watch for them, & be strong. They have the

world to lose. The world is yours.
Move in it as you wish,
& be strong. Yes. Be strong.

—Detroit, February 9, 1967/
New Orleans, December 4, 1995/
Amsterdam, December 2, 2002

"Love"

> Once you become aware
> of this force for unity in life, you can't ever
> forget it. It becomes part
> of everything you do.
>
> In that respect, this is an extension
> of A LOVE SUPREME
> since my conception of that force
> keeps changing shape. My goal
>
> on meditating on this
> through music, however,
> remains the same. And that is
> to uplift people,
>
> as much as I can. To inspire them
> to realize more & more of their capacities
> for living meaningful lives. Because there certainly is
> meaning to life.
>
> —John Coltrane

I said to my brother & my wife once
the first time we all took acid, sitting out in the car
in front of 4825 [John C. Lodge], & before we took the car
trip all the way to Chicago to hear Trane

still full of the acid, that we would see the day
after the post-Western revolution
when the language would work again
strictly as a function of the body, its

glow & gesture, that after enough of us had eaten the acid
we could then speak through our cells
as our cells, that the language would be stripped
of all negative force, & the new poetry

would burn itself down
to just one word, & the poets would say it
& everybody would be a poet, & the word would burn
        itself
into every body's meat, & people would hold hands &
        smile,

& the word would fill the world
vibrating through it, & through every part of it
merging all persons into ONE, the force for
unity in life, & that ONE to be taken

the only way possible, in a totally
post-Western sense, all senses brought together
in the flesh, & the world seen only one possible way,
AS IT IS, & the word would be there to

speak for us, & for the world, & Jimmy Garrison
would be playing bass, yes he would, & the music
would BE the word, & the voice of John Coltrane
would speak the word through the world

through the bell of his horn, & the word he sang would
pass through our eyes, through every cell
in our lovely meat, & yes, the vibrations
would BE the world

& the word is LOVE
Yes it is
The Word is LOVE
& it is here on earth

Yes it is
& the World is LOVE
Yes it is
O people, Yes it is

—Detroit
February 9, 1967
7:40 am

"The Father & The Son & The Holy Ghost"

During the year 1957 I experienced,
by the grace of God, a spiritual awakening
which was to lead me to a richer, fuller,

more productive life. At that time,
in gratitude, I humbly asked
to be given the means & privilege

to make others happy through music.
I feel this has been granted
through his grace. ALL PRAISE TO GOD.

I believe in all religions.

—John Coltrane

The tongue of fire
was always there, it IS
always there, & it will
all ways be

In the beginning was the word, & the word
is Love, & the word
is made flesh, in the daily struggle
to give birth to our selves

at every movement of the breath. And the breath is Love,
& descends into our flesh. John Coltrane is the Father,
as we all are. Pharaoh Sanders
IS the Holy Ghost. And the word is Love,

& the word is made flesh, & lo,
the Son is born, the Sun is our god, the Sun
is the energy / source, we are all agents of the Sun,
we will work to bring light to all persons,

we are the white light
burning through our flesh, it burns
through our eyes, we walk through the world
& the world is ours, ALL PRAISE TO THE GODS

we all of us are, & we are gods only
as we are HUMAN, our term is the universe,
we are humans in the world
& our sentence is LOVE, our sentence

is flesh, we are what we are
& we had best make
use of our selves, "Pharaoh is a man
of large spiritual reservoir. He's always trying

to reach out to truth. He's trying to allow his spiritual self
to be his guide. He's dealing, among other things,
in energy, in integrity, in essences. He is dealing
in the human experience," & the human experience

is the birth of the word which is Love
into flesh which is man, "a song is heat," the tongue of fire
moves through the meat & out through it, "Sound
is fire. As love

is" what the song is
& the song is the meat
screaming in the heat of the moment,
"You just keep going all the way, as

deep as you can," into the meat, AAHHHHHHH,
the light flashes, & we are happy only
as we keep the light flashing in our flesh,
through our eyes, out the mouth, the mouth spreads

in beautiful smiles, we dance in the sun
& the energy flashes through us, "you keep trying
to get right down to the crux," & the crux keeps moving,
it is the breath,

I celebrate the Sun
I celebrate the holy flesh
I celebrate the divine wind which is the breath
I celebrate the instant & eternal birth of the Father

I celebrate the birth of the word which is Love into flesh
which is the Son
I celebrate the Sun
I celebrate the Holy Ghost

I celebrate the spontaneous scream of meat energy
which is Pharaoh Sanders the tongue of fire in the flesh
I celebrate the talking in tongues which is language
which is Love

I celebrate the birth of the word in my flesh
& the word is Love
& the song has no end
& the song is Love

—Detroit
February 9, 1967
9:45 am/
Amsterdam, May 20, 2007

"Compassion"

There is never any end.
There are always new sounds to imagine, new feelings
to get at. And always, there is the need to keep purifying
these feelings & sounds so that we can really see

what we've discovered in its pure state. So that we can see

more & more clearly what we are. In that way, we can give
to those who listen
the essence, the best of what we are…

—John Coltrane

The sun is always where it is, it does not "come
up in the morning," we are just turned a-
way from it each day, & even at night
we can feel its energy reflected at us, I mean

we don't have to look for anything in the universe,
everything's THERE, what is search but
going after what ALREADY EXISTS, or
"tuning in" to what is already happening, yes,
energy & love are our natural state, & we become
unnatural when we lose sight of what we are, & of what
all humans are, & try to turn the world
against itself, when we will not see the world & its people

as exactly what they are but put some
alien measure to them, compassion is no more than love
brought to bear in every instance, I mean
EVERY instance, all of us have histories

& if you can SEE the world as it is you will not ig-
nore these histories, people will not act wrongly only a-
gainst their natural state, & their actions
are never random, the act of compassion is the act

of finding out WHY people do
the things they do. And is it never easy,
energy does have to be used "morally," which is to say

humanly, I mean to get back to our
natural state my fellow humans, & since the Love is there
it just has to be used, just to bring the world
into its own focus,

FIND the world,
it's right there in
front of you, & if you need help, well,
500 mikes will help you clear the

shit away, try it & see, & what you will find
is only beautiful humans,
you will love them,
love & compassion will rule,

you will be happy,
& if that ain't enough, then,
John Coltrane will be playing too
Just for you

—Detroit
February 9, 1967, 12 noon/
Amsterdam, May 20, 2007

"Serenity"

> *I am always searching; I think now*
> *that we're at the point of finding.*

—John Coltrane

So we find the world at last, & are at
one with it, & it is good, there is
no thing to fear, our peace comes through

our acceptance, our acknowledgement
of the way things are, but that only
in only the most contemporary sense, as this

music is current, I mean to make use of
the contemporary possibilities, to do everything
you can do

to love the world & its people,
they help your help,
you are serene with the knowledge

the resolution for & pursuance of
love in all forms
as there is only one form,

the Total,
& the Psalm of your self
is where you can be found—

& you are Love born
human in the world
at one with all humans

serene in your skin

—Detroit
February 11, 1967/
Amsterdam, May 21, 2007

IV

THE HEAVYWEIGHT CHAMPION

John Coltrane
THE HEAVYWEIGHT CHAMPION
The Complete Atlantic Recordings
Rhino Records 7-CD Box Set

There is no time frame around the music of John Coltrane. Okay, it was created during a period of 25 years, between 1942 and mid-1967, and the music in this 7-CD boxed set of John Coltrane's complete recorded output for Atlantic Records was all cut very specifically during the two years between 1959 and 1961. But Trane's music is timeless, for the ages, and it'll sound just as good 200 years from today as it did the day it was recorded.

So, there's no hurry to get this box in your home. Save your money, wait and pray, and when you do enter the musical world delineated on these discs, something utterly wonderful will be there waiting for you, just as it's been sitting there waiting almost 35 years to be collected, collated and presented in strict chronological order like this.

John Coltrane's Atlantic recordings saw the light of day in somewhat different order. After spending the previous three years making every possible kind of session for Prestige, Blue Note, Bethlehem, Savoy, Jubilee, and other small labels (his recordings for Prestige alone run to more than 18 compact discs), Trane determined upon signing an exclusive contract with Atlantic at the beginning of 1959 to take full control of his music, strike out on his own as a bandleader, and present a series of albums of his original works as coherent statements of intent and execution.

The first, released in January 1960, was called *Giant Steps* and featured Trane with Tommy Flanagan, Paul Chambers and Arthur Taylor in a carefully tailored program of new Coltrane compositions: "Giant Steps," "Cousin Mary," "Countdown," "Spiral," "Syeeda's Song Flute," "Mr. P.C." and "Naima," a gorgeous ballad that utilized the Miles Davis rhythm section of Wynton Kelly, Paul Chambers, and Jimmy Cobb.

Giant Steps followed closely upon the release of Miles Davis's monumental album, *Kind of Blue*, recorded for Columbia Records, which had established Coltrane as the pre-eminent tenor saxophonist of his generation. Cloaked in a striking red and white cover, *Giant Steps* cooked from beginning to end, thrusting Trane's gigantic sound, indefatiguable drive, and compositional genius even further into the forefront of modern music.

While listeners in 1960 were struck by the exceptional power and coherence of Coltrane's statement on the *Giant Steps* album, the posthumous release of the *Alternate Takes* album in 1975 revealed the full extent of his preparations for recording his first Atlantic disc. The first quartet he assembled, with Cedar Walton on piano, bassist Paul

Chambers, and Lex Humphries on drums, cut a session on March 26, 1959 which Coltrane completely rejected.

He regrouped with Flanagan and Taylor for the May 4-5, 1959 sessions that resulted in the *Giant Steps* album, and even then there were two completed takes each of "Countdown," "Syeeda's Song Flute," and "Cousin Mary." This meticulous preparation was to characterize his ground-breaking work with Atlantic and paid off beautifully at each session.

Coltrane struck next with a brilliant set called *Coltrane Jazz*, seven more musical gems recorded with the Miles Davis rhythm section and a single selection, "Village Blues," which introduced his 1960 quartet with McCoy Tyner, Steve Davis & Elvin Jones. *Coltrane Jazz* is one of Trane's finest pre-Impulse albums with its lilting swing, precision of statement, and great originals like "Some Other Blues," "Like Sonny," "Fifth House," and "Harmonique." The obscure pop tunes—"Little Old Lady," the gorgeously played "I'll Wait and Pray," and Trane's lusty reading of "My Shining Hour"—only enhance the handsome program of Coltrane compositions.

But it was "Village Blues" that turned people's heads early in 1961 when *Coltrane Jazz* was released. Here was something completely fresh and new from the well-established tenor saxophonist: a wholly distinctive rhythm section sound with the leader featured on top of a slow droning blues limned by Tyner's chording piano and underlined by the stark, complex polyrhythms of Elvin Jones.

Unknown to contemporary listeners, the new approach glimpsed on "Village Blues" had already come and gone in the studios of Atlantic Records. Recorded at three mammoth sessions cut between October 21-26, 1960, which produced nineteen masters—13 Coltrane originals and six radical reworkings of pop tunes—and eventually filled three entire Atlantic albums, the music of the Coltrane-Tyner-Steve Davis-Elvin Jones quartet served basically as a transitional vehicle which would take Trane to the next level of his development as a soloist, bandleader, and recording artist. Indeed, by the time he cut his final session for Atlantic in May 1961, Coltrane was featuring his new musical partner, Eric Dolphy, in a program of long Moorish- and West African-inspired modal works ("Ole," "Dahomey Dance") and working with Dolphy and Tyner in preparing orchestral arrangements of recent compositions for his first Impulse Records date, issued as *Africa/Brass*.

But it was the first full release by the new John Coltrane Quartet, an album titled *My Favorite Things*, that etched a new template for post-modern jazz and propelled Trane into the hearts of the record-buying public. Released in March 1961, this collection of standards and show tunes—done up in hypnotic, trance-inducing fashion and driven by the amazing percussive artistry of Elvin Jones— captured the public imagination in a big way, eventually selling over a million copies.

Most stunning was Trane's long workout on the title track, a bit of Rodgers & Hammerstein fluff from *The Sound of Music* then associated with Mary Martin and the Broad- way cast, on which Coltrane featured his newly-acquired soprano saxophone. No one who heard this record was untouched by its simplicity, grace, and emotional depth, and it brought Coltrane to the attention of a much wider audience than he had hitherto enjoyed—an audience which would sustain him and his bands through the last six turbulent years of his residency here on earth.

My Favorite Things stayed on the turntables of America's jazz lovers throughout 1961, bringing endless pleasure with Trane's absolutely idiosyncratic readings of "Summertime," "But Not For Me," the lovely ballad "Ev'ry Time We Say Goodbye," and the irresistible title tune. But Coltrane had moved a long way in a very short time, and the contrast between the old Trane and the new was perfectly effected when Atlantic countered the Impulse release of *Africa/Brass* at the end of 1961 with a straight- ahead, post-bop-and-blues set featuring the saxophonist with vibraharpist Milt Jackson and an unabashedly conservative rhythm section of Hank Jones, Paul

Chambers, and the MJQ's Connie Kay, recorded at Trane's first session for Atlantic on January 15, 1959.

Africa/Brass took *My Favorite Things* and Coltrane's next Atlantic release, *Ole' Coltrane*, issued in February 1962, another giant step further down the road toward the utter freedom of expression and articulation of emotion he was then beginning to realize onstage in the company of Eric Dolphy, McCoy Tyner, Jimmy Garrison and Elvin Jones. Trane's powerful tenor playing on "Africa" and "Blues Minor," raging over a large, rumbling orchestra directed by Dolphy and Tyner, lifted the music to new heights of emotional expression and instrumental virtuosity, and his soprano saxophonics on the old English folk tune, "Greensleeves," firmly established the straight horn as something a whole generation of reed players would have to come to terms with.

Once Coltrane's Impulse records starting coming out— *Africa/Brass*, *Live at the Village Vanguard*, *Coltrane*, and the rest—his remaining Atlantic releases served the same function as the Miles Davis Quintet's series of albums— *Cookin'*, *Relaxin'*, *Workin'*, and *Steamin'*—issued by Prestige after Miles had gone on to Columbia Records in 1956: they documented the immense artistic achievement of one of the greatest small jazz bands of all time as its members committed their current repertoire—literally, the state of their art—to recording tape over three long days in the studio.

The material recorded contemporaneously with the program of standards issued as *My Favorite Things* made up the next two Atlantic LPs. *Coltrane Plays the Blues* — released in July 1962, around the same time that *Live at the Village Vanguard* came out on Impulse—collected a series of blues performances by the quartet which took this basic African-American song form past the existing limits of musical abstraction, yet consistently filled it with as much feeling and fundamental compassion as a performance by Robert Johnson or Muddy Waters.

Coltrane's Sound, issued in June 1964, collects most of the rest of the masters from the October 1960 sessions, including the extremely urgent "The Night Has a Thousand Eyes," Trane's recasting of "Body and Soul" in his own image, and four stellar originals: "Liberia," "Central Park West," "Satellite," and "Equinox." While this music sounded hopelessly dated at the time of its release—it had to compete with the epochal *Coltrane Live At Birdland*, then just out on Impulse—it is immensely rewarding when heard in the actual context of its creation, as you may do by playing Discs 3, 4, 5, and 6 from the Atlantic box.

The last Atlantic album to come out before Trane's untimely demise in July 1967 shocked attentive Coltrane worshippers at the same time it filled in an overlooked sector of the map of the saxophonist's development.

Titled *The Avant-Garde: John Coltrane & Don Cherry*, this April 1966 release presented Trane in the company of the Ornette Coleman band of July 1960, struggling alongside pocket trumpeter Don Cherry to make sense of some of Ornette's most brilliant early works: "Invisible," "The Blessing," "Focus on Sanity." Monk's "Bemsha Swing" is also on the program, plus Don Cherry's "Cherryco," and the rhythm section is Edward Blackwell with Charlie Haden or Percy Heath.

The Avant-Garde clearly illuminates the parameters of Coltrane's quest to make something new and uniquely his own between the severe classicism of *Giant Steps* and *Coltrane Jazz* and the hyponotic intensity of *My Favorite Things, Coltrane Plays the Blues, Coltrane's Sound*, and *Ole' Coltrane*. He'd already explored in depth the musical worlds of Dizzy Gillespie, Miles Davis, and Thelonious Monk, recorded with George Russell and Cecil Taylor, wood-shedded with Yusef Lateef and John Gilmore (of the Sun Ra Arkestra), studied African drumming with Olatunji and Indian ragas with Ravi Shankar (after whom he was to name his son), and now completed his investigations into outside sources with a full-scale immersion into the music of Ornette Coleman, Don Cherry and Edward Blackwell. When he formed his master quartet and entered the Atlantic studios on October 21, 1960 to record "Village

Blues" and "My Favorite Things," John Coltrane was finally ready to put his own ineradicable mark on the shape of jazz to come.

Well, it's all here in *The Heavyweight Champion*, a box of music that will bring its listeners countless hours of joy and enlightenment. The music is presented in exactly the order in which it was recorded, alternate takes as well as masters, and there's a stunning cloth-bound booklet of information, photographs and testimony to answer your every question about the Atlantic years of the great master saxophonist, composer, and bandleader. The previously issued material takes up six full CDs, and then there's a bonus disc of session chatter, outtakes, and alternates that will put you straight in the studio with John Coltrane and his band as they perfect their approach to such all-time classics as "Giant Steps," "Naima," and "Like Sonny."

Let us briefly express our appreciation to the late Nesuhi Ertegun, who produced the Atlantic sessions; Joel Dorn, producer of this compilation; Lewis Porter, who assisted in its production and contributed the superb set of booklet notes; and Patrick Milligan, for his fine discography of the Atlantic sessions and for pulling this incredible project together. It joins the Ornette Coleman box of complete Atlantic recordings as essential and much-needed documents of the development of the contemporary creative music known as jazz. And may we suggest, while you're at it: *The Complete Atlantic Recordings of Charles Mingus*. Oh yeah!

—New Orleans
October 20, 1995

NOTES & ACKNOWLEDGEMENTS

This book was first assembled in 1987
in commemoration of the birthday
of John Coltrane—

Born in Hamlet, North Carolina,
September 23, 1926
Died July 17, 1967—

& to mark the passing of 20 years
since his spirit moved on
to some higher plane.

With two exceptions, each of these works
is titled after a song or an album
recorded by John Coltrane.

For your listening pleasure, & to provide
the proper sound track for this book,
these sources will yield the appropriate music:

"some other blues" & "like Sonny,"
from *Coltrane Jazz*
Atlantic Records (recorded 1959)

"blues to elvin" & "blues to you"
from *Coltrane Plays The Blues*
Atlantic Records (recorded 1960)

"spiritual" from
Coltrane Live At The Village Vanguard
Impulse Records (recorded 1961)

"the drum thing"
from *Crescent*
Impulse Records (recorded 1964)

"Welcome" & "Vigil"
from *Kulu Se Mama*
Impulse Records (recorded 1965)

Coltrane Live At Birdland, A Love Supreme &
The John Coltrane Quartet Plays
Impulse Records (recorded 1964 & 1965)

"Song of Praise"
from *The John Coltrane Quartet Plays*
Impulse Records (recorded 1965)

"Consequences"
from *Meditations*
Impulse Records (recorded 1966)

The exceptions are "Homage To John Coltrane"
which is set to music from *Coltrane*
Impulse Records (recorded 1962)

& "I Talk With The Spirits,"
a Rahsaan Roland Kirk title from
I Talk With The Spirits on Mercury Records

Most of the work in this book
has previously been published
in many books & magazines, including:

"Homage To John Coltrane," "blues to elvin,"
"some other blues," "like Sonny," "the drum thing"
in *This Is Our Music* (Artists Workshop Press, 1965)

"Song of Praise" & *The John Coltrane
Quartet Plays* in *Fire Music: A Record*
(Artists Workshop Press, 1966)

Meditations: A Suite For John Coltrane
was published at the Artists Workshop Press, 1967
& by Cary Loren at BookBeat in a facsimile edition, 2007

"Song of Praise" was also issued
as a holiday broadside/card by the
Artists Workshop Press, December 1965

Coltrane Live At Birdland, Crescent & *A Love Supreme*
were "record reviews" for *Jazz* magazine,
September 1964, March 1965 & April 1965

The John Coltrane Quartet Plays
was a "record review" for *Sounds & Fury*,
October 1965

*Cecil Taylor, John Coltrane & Archie Shepp
at the downbeat Jazz Festival* was a "concert review"
for *Change/1*, Winter 1965-66

"spiritual" was published by Pat Smith
in *Notus* magazine, Ann Arbor,
Volume 1, Number 1 (Fall 1986)

"spiritual" & "consequences" also appear in
"We Just Change the Beat": Selected Poems
(Ridgeway Press, 1988)

The Heavyweight Champion was published
as a "record review" in the *Heartland Journal*,
Chicago, Fall 1995

I—HOMAGE TO JOHN COLTRANE
was issued as most of *Full Moon Night*
by Elik Press, 2007, with an essay by Dennis Formento

AS REAL AS THEY ARE

The enthusiasm of youth is the shock of first discovery. For those of us familiar with either the *eminence gris* of the 21st century underground, or the manager of the MC 5, here is another, younger man to contemplate.

1965: with the killing in Vietnam only recently come to the attention of Americans ("a long and murderous year,") the war at home intensified against the human rights of African Americans, and former allies found themselves separated from each other by the forces of no-good. In response, more radical expressions surged into their mouths. New allegiances had to be forged, new musics had to express these feelings, new poetries were created to take the study of consciousness deeper.

These poems came during a time when revolutions in literature, music, the press, and recording would make world-changing art available to millions of people. Sinclair and a couple of dozen artists, writers, and musicians, founded Detroit Artists Workshop Society on November 1st, 1964. The Artists Workshop Press published *WORK* literary journal, *Change, Whe're, Free Poems Among Friends*, and the *Collected Artists Worksheets* (http://www.detroitartistsworkshop.org/).

In the year that many of these poems were composed, John was a featured reader at the Berkeley Poetry Conference, the summit conference of American outsider poetry. He was sponsored by Robert Creeley, another young jazz fanatic already established as a major poet. Allen Ginsberg was there, just back from a trip around the world, as was his rival for the "president of poetry," the great Charles Olson.

While Sinclair's tight lines of these are somewhat reminiscent of the late Mr. Creeley's, they forego his skeptical introspection for an ecstatic, gregarious, tone. In these poems, Sinclair holds nothing back.

In *SONG OF PRAISE*, we're at the meeting of the young idealist with the very real jazz genius, the younger man's expectations about his idol's inner life, and how he dreamed:

> of touching them, the musicians,
> as they walked off the stand, & moved past us,
>
> smiling, toward some secret place
> we would never go. & loved them always
> for a simple nod, as if we were really real.
> we needed them to speak to us
>
> of pure revolution. to put down their saxophones
> & spout pure poetry, or our lives
> weren't shit.
>
> (*"blues to you"*)

Sinclair sings,

> "let my

> poems be a
> graph of me," & with
> the poems, what other
> actions (gestures) i make.

> *("some other blues")*

He wanted to write "a true song of ourselves": echoing Walt Whitman, destroying barriers not only between individuals but between racial groups. "Oh, we were young / and made of America." Sinclair fashioned a song of the America of equality that Whitman loved, not the one the bard feared, that "fabled damned of nations," plundering the dark skinned peoples of the Americas and Africa.

Sinclair often credits Amiri Baraka, then still known as LeRoi Jones, for giving him a perspective on the aesthetics of jazz, and on race in America. In music, the thing to do, as Baraka wrote in his review of the Coltrane Village Vanguard disks, is to "reveal beauty, common or uncommon, uncommonly." Both men saw an opportunity to make that uncommon experience a common one to newly-liberated heads, willing for a moment to open themselves to uncustomary experience. We are born without prejudice, and to try to return to that innocence is a spiritual struggle. You've got to go way inside to get out. A moment's spiritual realization can put you on a trajectory that will carry you a lifetime. The spiritual struggle carries with it a responsibility to the people around us: see Trane's comment on the song, "Alabama" written not long after the infamous church bombing in Birmingham: "It represents, musically, something that I saw down there translated into music from inside me."

Nat Hentoff, in his notes on Trane and Pharoah Sanders, said the two were playing "as if ... with the gift of tongues." Insights/insides of such force that they had to leave ordinary musical language. "Turbulence naked as the self can be brought to be." This is exactly the beat aesthetic as exemplified by such pioneers as Allen Ginsberg and Bob Kaufman, the San Francisco street poet who best embodied the ethic of Beat.

John challenged his readers and listeners "If you can't / make these changes / make yr own" (*"some othe blues"*). If you're unsatisfied with what I'm doing, he says, do it yourself. The "change of the century" (a notion cribbed from Ornette's record) was maybe to make art "our" own way, direct and "out" when it was called for, going inside oneself, all the way back to the most archaic truths of human expression as they were first played on bone flutes over 15,000 years ago. Ayler, Coltrane, Coleman— these and other players wrought new art out of a primal urge to shout, hum, wail, and caterwaul.

Sinclair said of *A Love Supreme* that it "extends the limits of consciousness as far as they will go," suggesting Ginsberg's dictum to "widen the field of consciousness."

And writing about the same record:

> Coltrane has moved into a freer, more open music
> than many of us had thought possible, for him. What
> he has done, now, is to begin to analyze emotional
> states, through his music. Up to this record he has
> moved mainly to create emotion, & to transmit it,
> thru energy, to you, to create an emotional involve-
> ment, there, out of your own energies, as listener.

Reminds this reader of Charles Olson's landmark essay,
"Projective Verse." John speaks directly of "The Big O's"
similar attempts in poetry:

> In his new "open" or "projective" music (to use two
> terms which the poet Charles Olson has applied to
> the analogous "movement" in contemporary Ameri-
> can poetry), Coltrane can make new forms that are
> direct extensions of his musical content. He no lon-
> ger (now that he's hip to it) has to try to fit his "con-
> tent" into pre-determined forms,…

In his *Homage to John Coltrane*, some poems begin
with echoes of the previous poem's end, some end in
parenthetical asides, linking one to the other in an open
sequence. Like *A Love Supreme*, it is an extended work,
breaking the conventional form of individuated poems or
songs.

Sinclair's vocabulary is rich; he says Trane's tones are
"full-blooded"—Trane "worries a phrase, strokes it,

caresses, pushes and pulls" and finally "makes love to them"–Sinclair's poetry reflects that sensuality, with notes like "deeply smoked pearls," a psychedelic richness of senses. *Crescent* is the candle burning in the brain that begins on a golden love note passed to a woman under a crescent moon.

Segue thirty-five years into the future with *The Heavyweight Champion*. Here Sinclair shifts into a new stance, professorial, no longer the youthful guerilla poet throwing bombs of psychedelic light into the arena, but a seasoned pro, 'fessing what he knows regarding the order, content, highlights & artistic advances of Trane's time.

> A new world
> is only a new mind.
> And the mind and the poem
> are all apiece.
>
>   –William Carlos Williams

A very "Modernist" notion, and it makes me think how modernist this Sinclair work is, with its faith in human progress, its spiritual awakening in a secular, revolutionary context.

It puts John deep inside a tradition beginning with Whitman, Williams, and Ezra Pound, and continuing through Charles Olson and Ginsberg. It then lands him square in the middle of the 60s with Ed Sanders, who "invented the language" of investigative poetry, a poetry as much of fact as of inspiration, in which one may know one's world as well as sing it. Sinclair sings it here, extending Coltrane's flurries into psychedelic transcendence.

–Dennis Formento

Turning People On: An Interview with John Sinclair

[The following is an excerpt from a conversation between Dave Brinks and John Sinclair which took place on the evening of Saturday, February 28, 2009 above the Gold Mine Saloon in the French Quarter, New Orleans. This interview was first published in *ArtVoices*, Issue 14, April 2009.]

Brinks: There's about eight hundred things I've always wanted to ask you, but one thing that really jumps into my head: we were talking about poet Robert Creeley a minute ago, who put together that book of poetry by Paul Blackburn, after Paul died, called *Against the Silences*, and how Creeley was thinking of Paul's documentary efforts of course —and his poetry, and how all that's just one bag— and in the preface to that book, Creeley states: "It's a very real life. The honor, then, is that one live it." So, that's pretty heavy, right, but then in 1964, you're 23 years old, and on November 1st you founded the Detroit Artists Workshop, and about six months later you're headed off to the now legendary Berkeley Poetry Conference of July 1965 where Ginsberg introduces you as one of four "Young American Poets." You're in great company, with poets Ed Sanders, Ted Berrigan, and Lenore Kandel; and you bring fresh-off-the-press copies with you of that first issue of your magazine *Work*, and your first book *This Is Our Music*—so my question is two words actually—aside from everything , and still today, because the conversation continues—"why poetry?"

Sinclair: I'll say it like Lenny Bruce said it, "Why not?" And remember Lenny also had that opinion about "Why use narcotics?" —"Why not?" I don't know man, I mean, poetry, Allen Ginsberg, Ferlinghetti, those were the first ones I read, and Kerouac's prose where poets were glorified, and I mean, the idea of being a poet was not something that was out there on the table, you had to find that one. And that's probably the same question my mother had, "Why poetry? John, couldn't you just write some songs or something you might get paid for?" —No, mom, you don't understand. But it was a noble cause. You felt these guys, once Ginsberg and Ferlinghetti had City Lights Books going, waving the flag, they were there—they got these little books out, they were like 75 cents, there was *Kora in Hell* by William Carlos Williams, there was *Gasoline* by Gregory Corso, *Paroles* by Jacques Prévert, I can see those things, and *Howl*, *Kaddish*, *Pictures of the Gone World*, they were just fucking perfect: Iconically, textually, visually.

Yeah, they put poetry—it wasn't like Robert Frost, or these cornballs I couldn't stand—it was a manly endeavor. These guys were also hanging out at night clubs with black people, listening to jazz, or smoking marijuana, following these narcotics addicts like Charlie Parker. It was just so appealing. And I got it listening to jazz right exactly at the same time. It came as a package to me. It was life in a different part of the social order from anything that had been proposed. They were actually creating poetry readings where they had a lot of fun. Fucking unbelievable, with Gary Snyder reading from what would become *Riprap*, and Michael McClure reading his incredible odes. That was just very, very attractive to me. And the more you looked into to it, the more you found. And then you get to Charles Olson and Robert Creeley. And that was the twin towers, real poetry. Not to say Ginsberg isn't real poetry because he is. But I mean Charles Olson is real poetry man, and he's a real poet. That was his identity and that was what he did. And the idea of that was overwhelming, that you would be a poet, and what would you do—you would write poems, and you would study it, and you would learn about things you were interested in, and then your poems would say what you had to say. And they would also provide thrills—rhythmic and intellectual and emotive thrills, ya know. It was like an R & B record, or a Soul record, but it was heavier in a way. It was farther out. It didn't rhyme. And there wasn't anyone who was going to play it on the radio. You had to type up stencils and run them off the mimeograph machine to disseminate these works. Those times were so exciting to pursue.

Brinks: I'd like to talk about your magazine *Work* and those early days, and also the whole idea of that title *Work*, but specifically in the Creeley aspect of things, that work is something that happens between people; and also with the knowledge of humanness which comes specifically from Olson's thinking.

Sinclair: It was also an exhortative: You work. It was a way of life. It was a concept that we were committed to. And this stuff was work, it wasn't just bullshit, it wasn't frivolous—I mean writing, it's work. And the Detroit Artists Workshop was where you did the work. And you did it together in a communal setting, or in a cooperative setting that was communal at best; and we also lived together, so we had to do that too. And like I said before we started, we sealed our fate in a way, and stated our intention, when we put the notice on our publications: COPYRIGHT IS OBSOLETE. We really believed that. And part of it was, ya know, there wasn't really any concept that you would ever be compensated for this. That was part of the work—that you would do this work, despite the fact that unlike regular work, you wouldn't get paid, and it would be its own reward. And you would turn people on, not so much to your works, but to a concept of work that they could adopt and give meaning to their lives. That was the exciting part—not so much that someone was reading one of your poems, although of course this gave you a certain satisfaction to get a response from an audience. But it was really about the whole experience, and everybody involved, and the fact that we were making something in life in America that wasn't like what it was supposed to be. It wasn't about money, it wasn't about ego, it wasn't about career advancement. It was about doing the work, and doing it together, and having fun doing it, making it happen—that was fun shit.

We did poetry readings every Sunday. We were like second-lines in New Orleans. On Sunday afternoon you went to the Artists Workshop, then there was a poetry reading, and some musicians played, and whatever books you had, you would bring, like Allen Ginsberg or Amiri Baraka (who went by LeRoi Jones at the time) and Diane di Prima—people who were your role models. You would want to have their books so the other people could have access to this, so they could be as elated by it as you were.

Turning people on was the core value of our whole thing really. We wanted to turn people on. We just wanted to turn 'em on to art, poetry, and jazz. Then we started taking acid, ya know—regularly, and in groups. And then you developed this messianic feeling: you wanted to turn everyone on to everything. And you'd say, man, this works, you know, you might really like to try this. What a trip that was. You see, we were so far out on the edge of the social order. And in those days at the Artists Workshop, we had already basically written off the idea that any regular people could get to any of this. We felt that the only people who were really qualified to accept and enjoy this work were people who had already made some sort of commitment to a bohemian approach to life. We used to run our own flyers off for our Sunday afternoon Artists Workshop events. We'd stand on the corner on the campus of Wayne State, and we'd only give them to people who had moustaches. You wanted to get people that were coming out of the same matrix as yourself, because maybe they would get some of this, and at the very least, they would have a good time with it 'cause they weren't looking for—I don't know, the Beach Boys. We were on a search and destroy mission, ha ha. I guess it's arrogant in a way, but I mean, arrogance was probably a big part of our epic ambiguity.

Additional Notes :
There is a companion CD entitled *SONG OF PRAISE Homage To John Coltrane* that features performances of the poems found in this book.

SONG OF PRAISE Homage to John Sinclair CD
$15.00 (Kosmic Cow Productions)

Purchase a copy at Amazon, CDbaby, iTunes, or other music outlets.

Available as well at Trembling Pillow Press: www.tremblingpillowpress.com,

and John Sinclair's Website: JohnSinclair.us

IN HIS OWN WORDS

Photo Courtesy of Jacques Morial: John Sinclair in Amsterdam
broadcasting live on *The John Sinclair Show*

(The following is an excerpt from John Sinclair's *On The Road* archives which can be found on his website JohnSinclair.us/ on-the-road.html. This archive chronicles his travels across the US and Europe over the past ten years performing and collaborating with poets and musicians. Sinclair is widely recognized by his contemporaries as the "hardest working poet in show business," and this introductory post captures an intimate snapshot which no traditional biography could.)

ON THE ROAD #01 - January 13, 2004 (Amsterdam)

I waited a long time to hit the road as a poet. Although this writer has followed faithfully the bardic path for more than 40 years, there were so many other things to do along the way, and I did them.

As a cultural activist I directed the Detroit Artists Workshop, the Allied Artists Association, Jazz Research Institute and Detroit Jazz Center. I managed the MC-5, Mitch Ryder & Detroit and other bands. I produced dance concerts at the Grande Ballroom, free concerts in the parks, the Ann Arbor Blues & Jazz Festivals, and countless left-wing benefits, community cultural events, jazz concerts and poetry readings.

I've booked bands, bought talent and done publicity for nightclubs, bars and concert halls, developed programs, written grants and raised funds for jazz artists and community arts organizations, and produced records by artists from the MC-5, Little Sonny and Deacon John to Sun Ra, Victoria Spivey and Roosevelt Sykes. I've been a panelist for the National Endowment for the Arts, a professor of Blues History at Wayne State University, director of the City Arts Gallery for the City of Detroit, a community radio programmer and producer of WWOZ's live broadcast from the New Orleans Jazz & Heritage Festival.

As a professional journalist I've written columns, features and reviews about jazz and blues, rock & roll and poetry for publications of all sorts, from obscure local papers to *downbeat* and *Playboy* magazine. I've published poetry books and journals, edited underground newspapers, arts quarterlies and blues magazines, and written liner notes for albums by artists from Louis Armstrong, the Art Ensemble of Chicago and Harold Melvin & the Blue Notes to Johnny Adams, the Wild Magnolias and the Re-Birth Brass Band.

As a political activist I fought the marijuana laws through Detroit LEMAR, the Amorphia organization and a five-year struggle in the courts of Michigan that cost me 2-1/2 years in prison before I won my case and got the old laws thrown out. I was the chairman of the White Panther Party and its successor, the Rainbow Peoples Party, battling Richard M. Nixon and his goons from the beginning of his administration to the bitter end. It was my court case challenging Nixon's national security wiretap program that produced the historic Supreme Court decision in U.S. vs. U.S. District Court that warrantless wiretaps would no longer be allowed.

There's much too much more to mention, but let it suffice to say that I've enjoyed a full and productive life in the arts and community affairs for more than four decades and helped raise four terrific daughters in the process. But I started my adult life as a poet, setting my verses to music and performing them with jazz musicians and blues guitarists, and it was always my intention one day to take my own show on the road and pursue my performing arts career in earnest.

In truth what performing I did was done mostly for fun until 30 years had passed, and I was well beyond my 50th year when my first album, *Full Moon Night*, was released in the middle of the 1990s. I had finally realized my lifelong dream of hearing my verses and musical arrangements realized to perfection by a wildly sympathetic team of serious players, cleanly recorded in the heat and clarity of public performance, and my years of work in the music business told me it was time now to follow the bardic call and hit the road for real.

Since 1995 I've criss-crossed the United States and western Europe, working through a vast time-tested network of old friends and new comrades to assemble bands of Blues Scholars and book myself into funky nightclubs, blues bars, art galleries, coffeehouses, churches, cultural centers, college auditoriums and music and poetry festivals from coast to coast to coast.

Living in New Orleans in the 1990s I got to collaborate with a lot of great musicians, playing duets with Earl Turbinton, Johnny Vidacovich, Willie Metcalf and Walter "Wolfman" Washington; guesting with the groups of Michael Ray, the Radiators, Rockin' Jake, Stavin' Chain, New Orleans Juice, Brotherhood of Groove and the Jazz Vipers; and doing special projects with Mark Bingham, James Andrews, Tuba Fats, the Forgotten Souls Brass Band and a host of others. I formed my own band of Blues Scholars anchored by guitarist Bill Lynn and drummer Mike Voelker, and we played all over town, from Margaritaville and the Mermaid Lounge to JazzFest and the House of Blues.

When I started travelling, however, it was a rare occasion when I could take my band from New Orleans on the road with me. There's not much money in the poetry racket under the best of circumstances, so I generally travel by myself, hooking up with musician friends and friends of friends wherever I go. The cast of characters is always changing and the music behind me changes with them, so my texts stay fresh for me because they sound different every night. Plus I get to play with a thrilling array of great musical friends and make new connections with outstanding players in their prime locations, and that adds a level of excitement that's hard to beat.

In America, my three strongholds outside of New Orleans are Detroit, Boston and Oxford, Mississippi. In Detroit I get to work with my two most favorite guitarists, Jeff "Baby" Grand and James McCarty; and original Motor City Blues Scholars Martin Gross, Johnny Evans and R.J. Spangler. Outstate I hook up with Brian Bowe & the Saugatuck Blues Scholars on the west coast of Michigan and a great band called Glowb in my home town of Flint. I work all over New England every Fall with Ted Drozdowski & the Boston Blues Scholars, and in Oxford I'm part of an ensemble called Afrissippi that features Senegalese guitarist, singer and griot Guelel Kuumba, blues guitarists Eric Deaton and Jeff Henson, and a rhythm section rooted in the music of the North Mississippi hill country.

In Los Angeles I get to play with fellow former Detroiters Wayne Kramer, Charles Moore, Phil Ranelin & Buzzy Jones; in San Francisco it's Black Mike Henderson, Steve Mackay & the cats; in Seattle with Henry Cooper & Chris Morda, the son of my old friend and partner, Domenick Morda. In New York City it's Dee Pop, Ras Moshe and the great Daniel Carter; in Philadelphia with Elliott Levin, Calvin Weston & the Big Tree band, Tyrone Hill & Noel Scott from the Sun Ra Arkestra; in D.C. with Tom Dodd & the cats at the Signal 66 Gallery; in Chicago with Nick Tremulus, Warren Leming and the late Jimmie Lee Robinson; in St. Louis with Tom Papa Ray and the legendary Bennie

Smith; and in Kansas City with the guys from the Little Hatch band. My homeboy Doug Kaufman of Nobody in Particular Presents puts a band together for me in Denver, and I've done dates on the East Coast with old friends like David Amram, Archie Shepp, Bob Moses, Charles Eubanks and T.J. Wheeler & the Smokers.

So the particular kaleidoscope of music encountered from night to night is always the high point of every tour, and the changing sound of my poems helps keep things interesting for everyone concerned. Of course, when one proposes "An Evening of Music & Verse," very few people really have any idea of what they're going to hear when they get there anyway, but by the end of the night our audiences always seem to be glad they came (or, as the saying goes, whatever their response was).

On top of the music, the audiences and the performances themselves, the other great thing about travelling the bardic path is the incredible community of people who light up the way and see to the poet's modest needs while I'm in their town. Starting on the East Coast, my personal angels include George Kucewicz & Cathy Salmons in Boston, Bruce Pingree in Portsmouth, Paul Lichter & David Snow in Portland, Pete Gerson in Burlington, Mark Fisher & Mary-Claire Wellingon in Marblehead, my sister Kathy in New Haven, Joe Rosen & Giorgio Gomelsky in New York City, Danny Collins, Tommy Hard and the cats at the Wig Warmer in Philadelphia, and Steve Lewis and Tom Dodd at the Signal 66 Gallery in DC.

In the Midwest I'm blessed with the concern and care of Mark Steuve in Cleveland, Steve Gebhardt & Ed Moss & Ron Esposito in Cincinnati, the great Maribel Restrepo, Matty Lee and my daughter Sunny in Detroit, Jeff Strouss & Al Campbell in Ann Arbor, Michael & Paige James and the incomparable Fritz Keilsmier in Chicago, Michael Castro in St. Louis and Roger Naber in K.C. Heading West it's Cary & Nancy Wolfson in Boulder, Doug Kaufman in Denver, Harry Duncans, Chinner Mitchell & Jim Epstein in San Francisco, Mike Henderson in Oakland, Emil Bacilla in Sebastopol, Judge Eric Labowicz & Paul deMark in northern California, Chris Morda and Johnny "Boudreau" Frenchette and Craig Norberg in Seattle.

In Los Angeles I'm in the loving care of Michael Simmons, Wayne & Margaret Kramer, Patrick Boissel & Suzy Shaw, and the one & only Earl Palmer. Chad Henson & Allison Borders make me welcome and keep me fed in Oxford, and then there are all my peoples in New Orleans: my daughters Celia & Chonita, Wallace Lester & Shannon McNally, Jerry Brock, Sylvester Francis, Dennis Formento, Barry Smith at the Louisiana Music Factory, Barry Kaiser & Mary Moses, Tom Morgan & Hild Creed and others way too numerous to mention.

These are the people who pick me up at the train station and take me to the airport, bring me into their homes, put me up in their spare bedroom or let me sleep on their couch, feed me and get me high. They help me set up my gigs, drive me there, introduce me to all the cool people they know, take me out to dinner afterwards and help see to my recreational needs. They're the amazingly sweetest of friends, but they're also fellow artists and journalists and educators and broadcasters and producers, and their lives pulsate within the nexus of creative activity and social consciousness in the places they live.

They're always doing things themselves, making things happen, and they know what's going on around them as well. I bring them news from our mutual friends and other scenes around the country and take their stories and concerns along with me to the next stop on the trail.

List of Titles by John Sinclair

BOOKS:

This Is Our Music (Detroit: Artists Workshop Press, 1965; BookBeat, 1998)

Fire Music: A Record (Detroit: Artists Workshop Press, 1966)

The Poem for Warner Stringfellow (Detroit: Artists Workshop Press, 1967; BookBeat, 2005)

Meditations: A Suite for John Coltrane (Detroit: Artists Workshop Press, 1967; BookBeat, 2005)

Music & Politics (with Robert Levin) (New York: Jazz Press, 1971)

Guitar Army: Street Writings/ Prison Writings (New York: Douglas/ World, 1972)

We Just Change The Beat: Selected Poems (Detroit: Ridgeway Press, 1988)

fly right—a monk suite (Detroit: privately published, 1991)

thelonius: a book of monk—volume one (Detroit: privately published, 1991)

Full Circle: Selected Poems (Burlington: minimal press, 1998)

PeyoteMind (Oak Park: BookBeat, 2001)

Fattening Frogs For Snakes: Delta Sound Suite (New Orleans: Surregional Press, 2002)

i mean you—a book for penny (Berkeley: PalOmino Press, 2005)

Va Tutto Bene (Viterbo, Italy: Stampa Alternative, 2006)

Guitar Army (2nd Ed) (Los Angeles: Feral House/ Process Books, 2007)

Guitar Army (Italian Trans.) (Viterbo, Italy: Stampa Alternative, 2008)

It's All Good: A John Sinclair Reader (London, Headpress, 2008)

Full Moon Night (Elik Press, 2007)

Sun Ra Interviews & Essays, ed John Sinclair (London: Headpress, 2010)

Guitar Army (French Trans.) (Paris: Rivages/ Rouge, 2010)

Sun Ra Interviews & Essays, ed John Sinclair (Spanish trans.) (Madrid: Libertos Editorial, 2011)

ALBUMS:

We Just Change The Beat (cassette, 1988) with the Blues Scholars

fly right—a monk suite (unissued, 1991) with Ed Moss, piano

thelonius: a book of monk—volume one (New Alliance Records, 1994)

Full Moon Night (Alive/ Total Energy Records, 1995) with the Blues Scholars

If I Could Be With You (Schoolkids Records, 1996) with Ed Moss & the Society Jazz Orchestra

Full Circle (Alive Records, 1997) with Wayne Kramer & the Blues Scholars

White Buffalo Prayer (Spyboy Records, 2000) with Wayne Kramer & the Blues Scholars

Underground Issues (Spyboy Records, 2000)

Steady Rollin' Man with the Boston Blues Scholars (triPup Records, 2000)

The Delta Sound (OkraTone/ Rooster Blues Reocrds, 2002) with the Blues Scholars (Fattening Frogs for Snakes, Vol. 1)

It's All Good (Fluxedo Records, 2002) with LangeFrans & Baas B/ Wayne Kramer & the Blues Scholars

PeyoteMind (Oak Park: BookBeat, 2002) with Mystery Island

No Money Down: John Sinclair's Greatest Hits, Vol. 1 (Big Chief Records, 2005)

It's All Good with LangeFrans & Baas B/ Wayne Kramer & the
Blues Scholars (Big Chief Records, 2005)

criss cross (Big Chief Records, 2005) with Mark Ritsema

Country Blues (No Cover Records, 2005) with the Blues Scholars
(*Fattening Frogs for Snakes, Vol. 2*)

Don't Start Me To Talking (Big Chief/ Hill Country Records, 2007)
with the Blues Scholars (*Fattening Frogs for Snakes, Vol.*

Tearing Down the Shrine of Truth & Beauty (LocoGnosis Records,
2008) with the Pinkeye Orchestra

Detroit Life (No Cover Records, 2009) with the Motor City Blues
Scholars

Viper Madness (No Cover Records, 2010) with the Planet D Nonet

Let's Go Get 'Em (MoSound Records, 2011) with the International
Blues Scholars

Honoring the Local Gods (2011) with Hollow Bones

SONG OF PRAISE Homage to John Coltrane (Kosmic Cow Prod.,
2011) with the Blues Scholars

Natural From Our Hearts (MoSound Records, 2012) with the Blues
Scholars (*Fattening Frogs for Snakes, Vol. 4*)

Colophon

The type for this text is Palantino. Palatino was created with the experienced penmanship of Hermann Zapf in 1949. Palatino's classical proportions have placed it among the most universally popular of all roman typefaces. Palatino was named after the sixteenth-century Italian writing master. The broad letters and inclined serifs of the Palatino font family evoke a Renaissance grace.

The first 26 copies of this book are lettered and signed.

This copy is letter _____

Titles from Trembling Pillow Press

I of the Storm by Bill Lavender

Olympia Street by Michael Ford

Ethereal Avalanche by Gina Ferrara

Transfixion by Bill Lavender

The Ethics of Sleep by Bernadette Mayer

Downtown by Lee Meitzen Grue

SONG OF PRAISE   Homage To John Coltrane by John
   Sinclair

Forthcoming Titles

*Untitled Writings From A Member of the Blank
   Generation* by Philip Good

Maniac Memories by Jim Gustafson

Full Tilt Boogie or What's The Point by Paul Chasse

Trembling
Pillow
PRESS

www.tremblingpillowpress.com